Sexing Hardy: Thomas Hardy and Feminism
by Margaret Elvy

Thomas Hardy's Jude the Obscure: A Critical Study
by Margaret Elvy

Thomas Hardy's Tess of the d'Urbervilles: A Critical Study
by Margaret Elvy

Stepping Forward: Essays, Lectures and Interviews
by Wolfgang Iser

Andrea Dworkin
by Jeremy Mark Robinson

German Romantic Poetry: Goethe, Novalis,
Heine, Hölderlin, Schlegel, Schiller
by Carol Appleby

Cavafy: Anatomy of a Soul
by Matt Crispin

Rilke: Space, Essence and Angels in the Poetry of Rainer Maria Rilke
by B.D. Barnacle

Rimbaud: Arthur Rimbaud and the Magic of Poetry
by Jeremy Mark Robinson

Shakespeare: Love, Poetry and Magic in Shakespeare's Sonnets and Plays
by B.D. Barnacle

Feminism and Shakespeare
by B.D. Barnacle

The Poetry of Landscape in Thomas Hardy
by Jeremy Mark Robinson

D.H. Lawrence: Infinite Sensual Violence
by M.K. Pace

D.H. Lawrence: Symbolic Landscapes
by Jane Foster

The Passion of D.H. Lawrence
by Jeremy Mark Robinson

Samuel Beckett Goes Into the Silence
by Jeremy Mark Robinson

In the Dim Void: Samuel Beckett's Late Trilogy:
Company, Ill Seen, Ill Said and Worstward Ho
by Gregory Johns

Andre Gide: Fiction and Fervour in the Novels
by Jeremy Mark Robinson

The Ecstasies of John Cowper Powys
by A.P. Seabright

Amorous Life: John Cowper Powys and the Manifestation of Affectivity
by H.W. Fawkner

Postmodern Powys: New Essays on John Cowper Powys
by Joe Boulter

Rethinking Powys: Critical Essays on John Cowper Powys
edited by Jeremy Mark Robinson

Thomas Hardy and John Cowper Powys: Wessex Revisited
by Jeremy Mark Robinson

Thomas Hardy: The Tragic Novels
by Tom Spenser

Julia Kristeva: Art, Love, Melancholy, Philosophy, Semiotics
by Kelly Ives

Luce Irigaray: Lips, Kissing, and the Politics of Sexual Difference
by Kelly Ives

Helene Cixous I Love You: The Jouissance of Writing
by Kelly Ives

Emily Dickinson: *Selected Poems*
selected and introduced by Miriam Chalk

Petrarch, Dante and the Troubadours: The Religion of Love and Poetry
by Cassidy Hughes

Dante: *Selections From the Vita Nuova*
translated by Thomas Okey

Rainer Maria Rilke: *Selected Poems*
translated by Michael Hamburger

Walking In Cornwall
by Ursula Le Guin

Hölderlin's Songs of Light

Selected Poems

Hölderlin's Songs of Light

Selected Poems

Friedrich Hölderlin

Translated by Michael Hamburger
Edited by Jeremy Mark Robinson

CRESCENT MOON

First published 2003. Second edition 2008. Third edition 2012.
Translation © Michael Hamburger 1966, 1980, 1994, 2003.
Introduction © Jeremy Mark Robinson 2003, 2008, 2012.

Design by Radiance Graphics.
Printed and bound in the U.S.A.
Set in Book Antiqua.

British Library Cataloguing in Publication data

Hölderlin, Friedrich, 1770-1843
Hölderlin's Songs of Light: Selected Poems. – (European Writers)
I. Title II Hamburger, Michael III. Robinson, Jeremy Mark
831.6

ISBN-13 9781861713339 (Pbk)

Crescent Moon Publishing
P.O. Box 1312
Maidstone, Kent
ME14 5XU, U.K.
www.crmoon.com

Contents

Acknowledgements

To Michael Hamburger;
David Gascoyne;
Anvil Press Poetry Ltd, London;
Routledge Ltd, London;
Cambridge University Press, Cambridge;
Insel Verlag, Frankfurt, Germany.

Anvil Press Poetry for permission to reprint from Michael Hamburger's translations in Friedrich Hölderlin, *Poems and Fragments*, Anvil Press Poetry, 1994.

These translations have previously appeared in *Poems and Fragments*, tr. Michael Hamburger, Routledge, 1966; *Poems and Fragments*, tr. Michael Hamburger, Cambridge Uni-versity Press, 1980; and *Poems and Fragments*, tr. Michael Hamburger, Anvil Press, 1994.

Hölderlin's Songs of Light

Friedrich Hölderlin

AN DIOTIMA

Schönes Leben! du lebst, wie die zarten Blüthen im Winter,
  In der gealterten Welt blühst du verschlossen, allein.
Liebend strebst du hinaus, dich zu sonnen am Lichte des
                                              Frühlings,
  Zu erwarmen an ihr suchst du die Jugend der Welt.
Deine Sonne, die schönere Zeit, ist untergegangen
  Und in frostiger Nacht zanken Orkane sich nun.

EHMALS UND JEZT

In jüngern Tagen war ich des Morgens froh,
  Des Abends weint' ich; jetzt, da ich älter bin,
    Beginn ich zweifelnd meinen Tag, doch
      Heilig und heiter ist mir sein Ende.

HYPERONS SCHIKSAALSLIED

Ihr wandelt droben im Licht
  Auf weichen Boden, seelige Genien!
    Glänzende Götterlüfte
    Rühren euch leicht,
      Wie die Finger der Künstlerin
      Heilige Saiten.

Schiksaallos, wie der schlafende
  Säugling, athmen die Himmlischen;
    Keusch bewahrt
    In bescheidener Knospe,
      Blühet ewig
      Ihnen der Geist,
        Und die seeligen Augen
        Bliken in stiller
        Ewiger Klarheit.

Doch uns ist gegeben,
  Auf keiner Stätte zu ruhn,
    Es schwinden, es fallen
    Die leidenden Menschen
      Blindlings von einer
      Stunde zur andern,
        Wie Wasser von Lippe
        Zu Lippe geworfen,
          Jahr lang ins Ungewisse hinab.

DES MORGENS

Vom Thaue glänzt der Rasen; beweglicher
   Eilt schon die wache Quelle; die Buche neigt
     Ihr schwankes Haupt und im Geblätter
       Rauscht es und schimmert; und um die grauen

Gewölke streifen röthliche flammen dort,
   Verkündende, sie wallen geräuschlos auf;
     Wie Fluthen am Gestade, woogen
       Höher und höher die Wandelbaren.

Komm nun, o komm, unde eile mir nicht zu schnell,
   Du goldner Tag, zum Gipfel des immels fort!
     Denn offner fliegt, vertrauter dir mein
       Aug, du Freudiger! zu, so lang du

In deiner Schöne jugendlich blikst und noch
   Zu herrlich nicht, zu stolz mor geworden bist;
     Do möchtest immer eilen, könnt ich,
       Göttlicher Wandrer, mit dir!

Des frohen übermüthigen du, daß er
   Dir gleichen möchte; seegne mir lieber dann
     Mein sterblich Thun und heitre wieder
       Gütiger! heute den stillen Pfad mir.

"GEH UNTER, SCHÖNE SONNE"

Geh unter, schöne Sonne, sie achteten
  Nur wenig dein, sie kannten dich, Heilg, nicht,
    Denn mühelos und stille bist du
      Über den mühsamen aufgegangen.

Mir gehst du freundlich unter und auf, o Licht!
  Und wohl erkennt mein Auge dich, herrliches!
    Denn göttlich stille ehren lernt' ich
      Da Diotima den Sinn mir heilte.

O du desHimmels Botin! wie lauscht ich dir!
  Dir, Diotima! Liebe! wie sah von dir
    Zum goldnen Tage dieses Auge
      Glänzend und dankend empor. Da rauschten

Lebendiger die Quellen, es athmeten
  Der dunkeln Erde Blüthen mich liebend an,
    Und lächelnd über Silberwolken
      Neigte sich seegnend herab der Aether.

DIE LIEBE

Wenn ihr Freunde vergeßt, wenn ihr die Euern all,
  O ihr Dankbaren, sie, euere Dichter schmäht,
    Gott vergeb' es, doch ehret
      Nur die Seele der Liebenden.

Denn o saget, wo lebt menschliches Leben sonst,
  Da die knechtische jezt alles, die Sorge zwingt?
    Darum wandelt der Gott auch
      Sorglos über denn Haupt uns längst.

Doch, wie immer das Jahr kalt und gesanglos ist
  Zur beschiedenen Zeit, aber aus weißem Feld
    Grüne Halme doch sprossen,
      Oft ein einsamer Vogel singt,

Wenn sich mälig der Wald dehnet, der Strom sich regt,
  Schon die mildere Luft leise von Mittag weht
    Zur erlesenen Stunde,
      So ein Zeichen der schönern Zeit,

Die wir glauben, erwächst einziggenügsam noch,
  Einzig edel und fromm über dem ehernen,
    Wilden Boden die Liebe,
      Gottes Tochter, von ihm allein.

Sei geseegnet, o sei, himmlische Pflanze, mir
  Mit Gesange gepflegt, wenn des ätherischen
    Nektars Kräfte dich nähren,
      Und der schöpfrische Stral dich reift.

Wachs und werde zum Wald! eine beseeltere,
Vollentblühende Welt! Sprache der Liebenden
Sei die Sprache des Landes,
Ihre Seele der Laut des Volks!

IHRE GENESUNG

Sich! dein Liebstes, Natur, leidet und shläft und du
  Alllesheilende, säumst? oder ihr seids nicht mehr,
    Zarte Lüfte des Aethers,
      Und ihr Quellen des Morgenlichts?

Alle Blumen der Erd, alle die goldenen
  Frohen Früchte des hains, alle sie heilen nicht
    Dieses Leben, ihr Götter,
      Das ihr selber doch euch erzogt?

Ach! schon athmet und tönt heilige Lebenslust
  Ihr im reizenden Wort wieder, wie sonst und schon
    Glänzt in zärtlicher Jugend
      Deine Blume, wie sonst, dich an,

Heilige Natur, o du, welche zu oft, zu oft,
  Wenn ich trauernd versank, lächelnd das sweifelnde
    Haupt mit Gaaben umkränzte,
      Jugendliche, nun auch, wie sonst!

Wenn ich altre dereinst, siehe so geb ich dir,
  Die mich täglich verjüngt, Allesverwandelnde,
    Deiner Flamme die Schlaken,
      Und ein anderer leb ich auf.

UNTER DEN ALPEN GESUNGEN

Heilige Unschuld, du der Menschen und der
Götter liebste vertrauteste! du magst im
Hauße oder draußen ihnen zu Füßen
    Sizen, den Alten,

Immerzufriedner Weisheit voll; denn manches
Gute kennet der Mann, doch staunet er, dem
Wild gleich, oft zum Himmel, aber wie rein ist
    Reine, dir alles!

Siehe! das rauhe Thier des Feldes, gerne
Dient und trauet es dir, der stumme Wald spricht
Wie von Alters, seine Sprüche zu dir, es
    Lehren die Berge

Heil'ge Geseze dich, und was nocht jezt uns
Vielerfahrenen offenbar der große
Vater werden heißt, du darfst es allein uns
    Helle verkünden.

So mit den Himmlischen allein zu seyn, und
Geht vorüber das Licht, und Strom und Wind, und
Zeit eilt hin zum Ort, vor ihnen ein stetes
    Auge zu haben,

Seeliger weiß und wünsch' ich nichts, so lange
Nicht auch mich, wie die Weide, fort die Fluth nimmt,
Daß wohl aufgehoben, schlafend dahin ich
    Muß in den Woogen;

Aber es bleibt daheim gern, wer in treuem
Busen Göttliches hält, und frei will ich, so
Lang ich darf, euch all', ihr Sprachen des Himmels!
Deuten und singen.

DER BLINDE SÄNGER

Remotus enim acer ab oculis mali labor
  Sophocles

Wo bist du, Jugendliches! das immer mich
  Zur Stunde wekt des Morgens, wo bist du, Licht!
    Das Hertz ist wach, doch bannt und hält in
      Heiligem Zauber die Nacht mich immer.

Sonst lauscht' ich um die Dämmerung gern, sonst harrt'
  Ich gerne dein am Hügel, und nie unsonst!
    Nie täuschten mich, du Holdes, deine
      Boten, die Lüfte, denn immer kanst du,

Kamst allbeseeligend den gewohnten Pfad
  Herein in deiner Schöne, wo bist du, Licht!
    Das Herz ist wieder wach, doch bannt und
      Hemmt die unendliche Nacht mich immer.

Mir grünten sonst die Lauben; es leuchteten
  Die BLumen, wie die eigenen Augen, mir;
    Nicht ferne war das Angesicht der
      Meinen und leuchtete mir und droben

Und um die Wälder sah ich die Fittige
  Des Himmels wandern, da ich ein Jüngling war;
    Nun siz ich still allein, von einer
      Stunde zur anderen und Gestalten

Aus Lieb und Laid der helleren Tage schafft
  Zur eignen Freude nun mein Gedanke sich,
    Und ferne lausch' ich hin, on nicht ein
      Freundlicher Retter vieleicht mir komme.

Dann hör oft die Stimme des Donnerers
    Am Mittag, wenn der eherne nahe kommt,
        Wenn ihm das Haus bebt und der Boden
            Unter ihm dröhnt und der Berg es nachhalt.

Den Retter hör' ich dann in der Nacht, ich hör'
    Ihn tödtend, den Befreier, belebend ihn,
        Den Donnerer vom Untergang zum
            orient eilen und ihm nach tönt ihr,

Ihm nach, ihr meine Saiten! es lebt mit ihm
    Mein Lied und wie die Quelle dem Strome folgt,
        Wohin er denkt, so muß ich fort und
            Folge dem Sicheren auf der Irrbahn.

Wohin? wohin? ich höre dich da und dort
    Du Herrlicher! und rings um die Erde tönts.
        Wo endest du? und was, was ist es
            Über den Wlken und o wie wird mir?

Tag! Tag! du über stürzenden Wolken! sei
    Willkomen mir es blühet mein Auge dir.
        O Jugendlicht! o Glük! das alte
            Wieder! doch geistiger rinnst du nieder

Do goldner Quell aus heiligem Kelch! und du,
    Du grüner Boden, friedliche Wieg'! und du,
        Haus meiner Väter! und ihr Lieben,
            Die mir begegneten einst, o nahet,

O kommt, daß euer, euer die Freude sei,
    Ihr alle, daß euch seegne der Sehende!
        O nimmt, daß euch ichs ertrage, mir das
            Leben, das Göttliche mir vom Herzen.

DICHTERMUTH

Sind denn dir nicht verwandt alle Lebendigen?
  Nährt zum Dienste denn nicht selber die Parze dich?
    Drum! so wandle nur wehrlos
      Fort durch's Leben und sorge nicht!

Was geschiehet, es sei alles geseegnet dir,
  Sei zur Freude gewandt! oder was könnte denn
    Dich belaidigen, Herz! was
      Da begegnen, wohin du sollst?

Denn, wie still am Gestad, oder in silberner
  Fernhintönender Fluth, oder auf schweigenden
    Wassertiefen der leichte
      Schwimmer wandelt, so sind auch wir,

Wir, die Dichter des Volks, gerne, wo Lebendes
  Um uns athmet und wallt, freudig, und jedem hold,
    Jedem trauend; wie sängen
      Sonst wir jedem den eignen Gott?

Wenn die Wooge denn auch einen der Muthigen,
  Wo er treulich getraut, schmeichlend hinunterzieht,
    Und die Stimme des Sängers
      Nun in blauender Halle schweigt;

Freudig starb er und noch klagen die Einsamen,
  Seine Haine, den Fall ihres Geliebtesten;
    Öfters tönet der Jungfrau
      Vom Gezweige sein freundlich Lied.

Wenn des Abends vorbei Einer der Unsern kömmt,
  Wo der Bruder ihm sank, denket er manches wohl
    An der warnenden Stelle,
      Schweigt und gehet gerüsteter.

HEIMKUNFT

an die verwandten

1

Drinn in den Alpen ists noch helle Nacht und die Wolke,
    Freudiges dichtend, sie dekt drinnen das gähende Thal.
Dahin, dorthin toset und stürzt die scherzende Bergluft,
    Schroff durch Tannen herab glänzet und schwindet ein
                                Stral.
Langsam eilt und kämpft das freudigschauernde Chaos,
    Jung an Gestalt, doch stark, feiert es liebenden Streit
Unter den Felsen, es gährt und wankt in den ewigen
                                Schranken,
    Den bacchantischer zieht drinnen der Morgen herauf.
Denn es wächst unendlicher dort das Jahr und die heilgen
    Stunden, die Tage, sie sind kühner geordnet, gemischt.
Dennoch merket die Zeit der Gewittervogel und zwischen
    Bergen, hoch in der Luft weilt er und rufet den Tag.
Jezt auch wachet und schaut in der Tiefe drinnen das
                                Dörflein
    Furchtlos, Hohem vertraut, unter den Gipfeln hinauf.
Wachstum ahnend, denn schon, wie Blize, fallen die alten
    Wasserquellen, der Grund unter den Stürzenden dampft,
Echo tönet umher, und die unermeßliche Werkstatt
    Reget bei Tag und Nacht, Gaaben versendend, den Arm.

2

Ruhig glänzen indeß die silberenen Höhen darüber,
    Voll mit Rosen ist schon droben der leuchtende Schnee.
Und noch höher hinauf wohnt über dem Lichte der reine
    Seelige Gott vom Spiel heiliger Stralen erfreut.
Stille wohnt er allein und hell erscheinet sein Antliz,
    Der ätherische scheint Leben zu geben geneigt,
Freude zu schaffen, mit uns, wie oft, wenn, kundig des
                                    Maases,
    Kundig der Athmenden auch zögernd und schonend der
                                    gott
Wohlgediegenes Glük den Städten und Häußern und milde
    Reegen, zu öffnen das Land, brütende Wolken, und euch,
Trauteste Lüfte dann, euch, sanfte Frühlinge, sendet,
    Und mit langsamer Hand Traurige wieder erfreut,
Wenn er die Zeiten erneut, der Schöpferische, die stillen
    Herzen der alternden Menschen erfrischt und ergreifft,
Und hinab in die Tiefe wirkt, und öffnet und aufhellt,
    Wie ers liebet, und jezt wieder ein Leben beginnt,
Anmuth blühet, wie einst, und gegenwärtiger Geist kömmt,
    Und ein freudiger Muth wieder die Fittige schwelt.

3

Vieles sprach ich zu ihm, denn, was auch Dichtende sinnen
    Oder singen, es gilt meistens den Engeln und ihm;
Vieles bat ich, zu lieb dem Vaterlande, damit nicht
    Ungebeten uns einst plözlich befiele der geist;
Vieles für euch auch, die im Vaterlande besorgt sind,
    denen der heilige Dank lächelnd die Flüchtlinge bringt,
Landesleute! für euch, indessen wiegte der See mich,
    Und der Ruderer saß ruhig und lobte die Fahrt.
Weit in des Sees Ebene wars Ein freudiges Wallen
    Unter den Seegeln und jezt blühet und hellet die Stadt
Dort in der Frühe sich auf, wohl her von schattigen Alpen

Kommt geleitet und ruht nun in dem Hafen das Schiff.
Warm ist das Ufer hier und freundlich offene Thale,
    Schön von Pfaden erhellt grünen und schimmern mich an.
Gärten stehen gesellt und die glänzende Knospe beginnt
                                    schon,
    Und des Vogels Gesang ladet den Wanderer ein.
Alles scheinet vertraut, der vorübereilende Gruß auch
    Scheint von Freuden, es scheint jegliche Miene verwandt.

4

Freilich wohl! das Gerburstsland ists, der Boden der
                                    Heimath,
    Was du suchest, es ist nahe, begegnet dir schon.
Und umsonst nicht steht, wie ein Sohn, am
                                    wellenumrauschten
    Thor' und siehet und sucht liebende Nahmen für dich,
Mit Gesang ein wandernder Mann, glükseeliges Lindau!
    Eine der gastlichen Pforten des Landes ist diß,
Reizend hinauszugehn in die vielversprechende Ferne,
    Dort, wo die Wunder sind, dort, wo das göttliche Wild
Hoch in die Ebnen herab der Rhein die verwegene Bahn
                                    bricht,
    Und aus Felsen hervor ziehet das jauchzende Thal,
Dort heinein, durchs helle Gebirg, nach Komo zu wandern,
    Oder hinab, wie der Tag wandelt, den offenen See;
Aber reizender mir bist du, geweihete Pforte!
    Heimzugehn, wo bekannt blühende Wege mir sind,
Dort zu besuchen das Land und die schönen Thale des
                                    Nekars,
    Und die Wälder, das Grün heiliger Bäume, wo gern
Sich die Eiche gesellt mit stillen Birken und Buchen,
    Und in bergen ein ort freundlich gefangen mich nimmt.

5

Dort empfangen sie mich. O Stimme der Stadt, der Mutter!
　　O du trifest, du regst Langegelerntes mir auf!
Dennoch sind sie es noch! noch blühet die Sonn' und die
　　　　　　　　　Freud' euch,
　　O ihr Liebsten! und fast heller im Auge, wie sonst.
Ja! das Alte noch ists! Es gedeihet und reifet, doch keines
　　Was da lebet und liebt, lässet die Treue zurük.
Aber das Beste, der Fund, der unter des heiligen Friedens
　　Bogen lieget, er ist Jungen und Alten gespart.
Thörig red ich. Es ist die Freude. Doch morgen und künftig
　　Wenn wir gehen und schaun draußen das lebende Feld
Unter den Blüthen des Baums, in den Feiertagen des
　　　　　　　　　Frühlings
　　Red' und hoff' ich mit euch vieles, ihr Lieben! davon.
Vieles ha' ich gehört vom großen Vater und habe
　　Lange geschwiegen von ihm, welcher die wandernde Zeit
Droben in Höhen erfrischt, und waltet über Gebirgen
　　Der gewähret uns bald himmlische Gaaben und ruft
Hellern Gesang und schikt viel gute Geister. O säumt nicht,
　　Kommt, Erhaltenden ihr! Engel des Jahres! und ihr,

6

Engel des Haußes, koomt! in die Adern alle des Lebens,
　　Alle freuend zugleich, theile das Himmlische sich!
Adle! verjünge! damit nichts Menschlichgutes, damit nicht
　　Eine Stunde des Tags ohne die Frohen und auch
Solche Freude, wie jezt, wenn Liebende wieder sich finden,
　　Wie es gehört für sie, schiklich geheiliget sei.
Wenn wir seegnen das Mahl, wen darf ich nennen und wenn
　　　　　　　　　wir
　　Ruhn vom Leben des Tags, saget, wie bring' ich den Dank?
Nenn' ich den Hohen dabei? Unschikliches liebet ein Gott
　　　　　　　　　nicht,

Ih zu fassen, ist fast unsere Freude zu klein.
Schweigen müssen wir oft; es fehlen heilige Nahmen,
   Herzen schlagen und doch bleibet die REde zurük?
Aber ein Saitenspiel leiht jeder Stunde die Töne,
   Und erfreuet vieleicht Himmlische, welche sich nahn.
Das bereitet und so ist auch beinahe die Sorge
   Schon befriediget, die unter das freudige kam.
Sorgen, wie diese, muß, gern oder nicht, in der Seele
   tragen ein Sänger und oft, aber die anderen nicht.

from DER TOD DES EMPEDOKLES

Zweiter fassung

In meine Stille kamst du liese wandelnd,
Fandst drinnen in der Halle Dunkel mich aus,
Du Freundlicher! du kanst nicht unverhoft
Und fernher, wirkend über der Erde vernahm
Ich wohl dein Wiederkehren, schöner Tag
Und meine Vertrauten euch, ihr schnellgeschäftgen
Kräfte der Höh! – und nahe seid auch ihr
Mir wieder, seid wie sonst ihr Glüklichen
Ihr irrelosen Bäume meines Hains!
Ihr ruhetet und wuch'st und täglich tränkte
Des Himmels Quelle die Bescheidenen
Mit Licht und Lebensfunken säte
Befruhtend auf die Blühenden der Aether. –
O innige Natur! ich habe dich
Vor Augen, kennest du den Freund noch
Den Hochgeliebten kennest du mich nimmer?
Den Priester, der lebendigen Gesang,
Wie frohvergoßnes Opferblut, dir brachte?

Dritte fassung

Euch ruf ich über das Gefild herein
Vom langsamen Gewölk, ihr heißen Stralen
Des Mittags, ihr Gereiftesten, daß ich
An euch den neuen Lebenstag erkenne.
Denn anders ists wie sonst! vorbei, vorbei
Das menschliche Bekümmerniß! als wüchen
Mir Schwingen an, so ist mir wohl und leicht
Hier oben, hier, und reich genug und froh
Und herrlich wohn' ich, wo den Feuerkelch
Mit Geist gefüllt bis an den Rand, bekränzt
Mit Blumen, die er selber sich erzog.

[...]

Ja! ruhig wohnen wir; es öffnen groß
Sich hier vor uns die heilgen Elemente.
Die Mühelosen regen immergleich
In ihrer Kraft sich freudig hier um uns.
An seinen vesten Ufern wallt und ruht
Das alte Meer, und das Gebirge steigt
Mit seiner Ströme Klang, es woogt und rauscht
Sein grüner Wald von Thal zu Thal hinunter.
Und oben weilt das Licht, der Aether stilt
Den Geist und das geheimere Verlangen.
Hier wohnen ruhig wir!

HÄLFTE DES LEBENS

Mit gelben Birmen hänget
Und voll mit wilden Rosen
Das Land in den See,
Ihr holden Schwäne,
Und trunken von Küssen
Tunkt ihr das Haupt
Ins heilignüchterne Wasser.

Weh mir, wo nehm' ich, wenn
Es Winter ist, die Blumen, und wo
Den Sonnenschein,
Und Schatten der Erde?
Die Mauern stehn
Sprachlos und kalt, im Winde
Klirren die Fahnen.

MNEMOSYNE

Dritte fassung

Reif sind, in Feuer getaucht, gekochet
Die frücht und auf der Erde geprüfet und ein Gesez ist
Daß alles hineingeht, Schlangen gleich,
Prophetisch, träumend auf
Den Hügeln des Himmels. Und vieles
Wie auf den Schultern eine
Last von Scheitern ist
Zu behalten. Aber bös sind
Die Pfade. Nemlich unrecht,
Wie Rosse, gehen die gefangenen
Element' und alten
Geseze der Erd. Und immer
Ins Ungebundene gehet eine Sehnsucht. Vieles aber ist
Zu behalten. Und Noth die Treue.
Vorwärts aber und rükwärts wollen wir
Nicht sehn. Uns wiegen lassen, wie
Auf schwankemm Kahne der See.

Wie aber liebes? Sonnenschein
Am Boden sehen wir und trokenen Staub
Und heimatlich die Schatten der Wälder und es blühet
An Dächern der Rauch, bei alter Krone
Der Thürme, friedsam; gut sind nemlich
Hat gegenredend die Seele\
Ein Himmlisches verwlundet, die Tageszeichen.
Denn Schnee, wie Majenblumen
Das Edelmüthige, wo
Es seie, bedeutend, glänzet auf
Der grünen Wiese
Der Alpen, hälftig, da, vom Kreuze redend, das

Gesezt ist unterwegs einmal
Gestorbenen, auf hoher Straß
Ein Wandersmann geht zornig,
Fern ahnend mit
Dem andern, aber was ist diß?

   Am Feigenbaum ist mein
Achilles mir gestorben,
Und Ajax liegt
An den Grotten der See,
An Bächen, benachbart dem Skamandros.
An Schläfen Sausen einst, nach
Der unbewegten Salamis steter
Gewohnheit, in der Fremd', ist groß
Ajax gestorben
Patroklos aber in des Königes Harnisch. Und es starben
Noch andere viel. Am Kithäron aber lag
Elevtherä, der Mnemosyne Stadt. Der auch als
Ablegte den Mantel Gott, das abendliche nachher löste
Die Loken. Himmlische nemlich sind
Unwillig, wenn einer nicht die Seele schonend sich
Zusammengenommen, aber er muß doch; dem
Gleich fehlet die Trauer.

TRANSLATIONS

TO DIOTIMA

Beautiful being, you live as do delicate blossoms in winter,
  In a world that's grown old hidden you blossom, alone.
Lovingly outward you press to bask in the light of the
                                 springtime,
  To be warmed by it still, look for the youth of the world.
But your sun, the lovelier world, has gone down now,
  And the quarrelling gales rage in an icy bleak night.

THEN AND NOW

In younger days each morning I rose with joy,
To weep at nightfall now, in my later years,
Though doubting I begin my day, yet
Always its end is serene and holy.

HYPERION'S SONG OF FATE

You walk above in the light,
  Weightless tread a soft floor, blessed genii!
    Radiant the gods' mild breezes
      Gently play on you
        As the girl artist's fingers
        On holy strings.

Fateless the Heavenly breathe
  Like an unweaned infant asleep;
    Chastely preserved
     In modest bud
      For ever their minds
       Are in flower
        And their blissful eyes
         Eternally tranquil gaze,
         Eternally clear.

But we are fated
  To find no foothold, no rest,
    And suffering mortals
     Dwindle and fall
      Headlong from one
       Hour to the next,
        Hurled like water
         From ledge to ledge
          Downward for years to the vague abyss.

IN THE MORNING

With dew the lawn is glistening; more nimbly now,
  Awake, the stream speeds onward; the beech inclines
    Her limber head and in the leaves a
      Rustle, a glitter begins; and round the

Grey cloud-banks there a flicker of reddish flames,
  Prophetic ones, flares up and in silence plays;
    Like breakers by the shore they billow
      Higher and higher, the ever-changing.

Now come, O come, and not too impatiently,
  You golden day, speed on to the peaks of heavens!
    For more familiar and more open,
      Glad one, my vision flies up towards you

While youthful in your beauty you gaze and have
  Not grown too glorious, dazzling and proud for me;
    Speed as you will, I'd say, if only
      I could go with you, divinely ranging!

But at my happy arrogance now you smile,
  That would be like you; rather, then, rambler, bless
    My mortal acts, and this day also,
      Kindly one, brighten my quiet pathway.

"GO DOWN, THEN, LOVELY SUN"

Go down, then, lovely sun, for but little they
   Regarded you, nor, holy one, knew your worth,
     Since without toil you rose, and quiet,
       Over a people for ever toiling.

To me, however, kindly you rise and set,
   O glorious light, and brightly my eyes respond,
     For godly, silent reverence I
       Learned when Diotima soothed my frenzy.

O how I listened, Heaven's own messenger,
   To you, my teacher! Love! How to the golden day
     These eyes transfused with thanks looked up from
       Gazing at you. And at once more living

The brooks began to murmur, more lovingly
   The blossoms of dark Earth breathed their scent at me
     And through the silver clouds a smiling
       Aether bowed down to bestow his blessing.

LOVE

If you drop an old friend, if, O you grateful ones,
   Your own poets you slight, slander and cheapen, may
     God forgive you, but always
       Honour lovers, respect their soul.

For, I ask you, where else humanly do men live
   Now that slavish one, Care, rules and compels us all?
     Therefore too has the God long
       Moved uncaring above our heads.

Yet no matter how cold, songless the year may be,
   When the season is due still from the field all white
     New green blades will be sprouting,
       Often one lonely small bird will sing,

When the woods all expand, slowly, the river stirs
   Milder breezes at last tenderly blow from the south,
     At the hour pre-elected,
       So, a sign of the better age

We believe in, unique thanks to her self-content
   Noble, pious, on soil hard as iron and waste,
     Love, the daughter of God, comes,
       Only his and from him alone.

You, then, heavenly plant, now let me bless, and be
   Ever tended with song, when the æthereal
     Nectar's energies feed you,
       Ripened by the creative ray.

Grow and be a whole wood! be a more soul-inspired,
Fully blossoming world! Language of lovers now
Be the language our land speaks,
And their soul be the people's lilt!

HER RECOVERY

Nature, look, your most loved drowses and ails, and you
   Dally, healer of all? Have you grown weak, then, tired,
     Gentle breezes of Aether,
       Limpid sources of morning light?

All the flowers of the earth, all the deep golden-hued
   Happy fruits of the grove, how can it be that all
     Fail to cure this one life which,
       Gods, you raised for your own delight?

Ah, already restored, holy desire to live
   Breathes and sounds in her talk, charming as ever, and
     Tenderly youthful your darling
       Gleams at you as she did before,

Holy Nature, the same who all too often when
   Sadness made me sink down, smiling would garland my
     Head with gifts, with your riches,
       Youthful Nature, now too restored!

Look, one day when I'm old, you that transmute all things
   And now daily renew youth in me, I will give
     To your flame the dead cinders
       And revive as a different man.

SUNG BENEATH THE ALPS

Innocence, you the holy, dearest and nearest
Both to men and to gods! In the house or
Out of doors alike to sit at the ancients'
                Feet it behoves you,

Ever contented wisdom yours; for men know
Much that's good, yet like animals often
Scan the heavens perplexed; to you, though, how pure are
                All things, you pure one!

Look, the rough grassland beast is glad to serve and
Trust you; mute though it be, yet the forest
Now as ever yields its oracles up, the
                Mountains still teach you

God-hallowed laws, and that which even now the
Mighty Father desires to make known to
Us the much experienced, you, and you only
                Clearly may tell us.

Being alone with heavenly powers, and when the
Light begins to pass by, and swiftly river,
Wind and time seek out the place, with a constant
                Eye then to face them –

Nothing more blessed I know, nor want, as long as
Not like willows me too the flood sweeps on, and
Well looked after, sleeping, down I must travel,
                Waves for my bedding;

Gladly, though, he will stay at home who harbours
Things divine in his heart; and you, all Heaven's
Languages, freely, as long as I may, I'll
                    Sing and interpret.

THE BLIND SINGER

Cruel woe has Ares lifted from our eyes
  Sophocles

Where are you, youthful herald who always once
  Would waken me at daybreak, where are you, light?
    The heart's awake, but always Night now
      Holds me and binds me with holy magic.

Once towards dawn I'd listen, was glad to wait
  For you upon your hillside, and never in vain!
    Nor ever did your messengers, the
      Breezes deceive me, for always, dear one,

You came, delighting all, in your loveliness,
  Came down the usual pathway; where are you, light?
    The heart's awake once more, but always
      Infinite Night now constricts me, binds me.

Once green the bowers would beckon to me; the flowers
  Would shine for me, would gleam like my own two eyes;
    Not distant from me were my loved ones'
      Faces and shone for me, up above me

And round the woods I saw, as they travelled on,
  The wings of heaven – then, in the time of youth;
    Now here I sit alone in silence
      Hour after hour and for only comfort

My mind devises shapes for itself, made up
  Of love and grief remembered from brighter days,
    And far I strain my hearing lest a

Kindly deliverer perhaps is coming.

Then often I can hear the great Thunderer's voice,
   At noon when he, the brazen one, draws most near,
     When his own house quakes, the foundations
       Under him boom and the hill repeats it.

The saviour then I hear in the night, I hear
   Him kill, the liberator, and give new life,
     From West to East I hear the Thunderer
       Quickly sweep on, and it's him you echo,

My strings! With him, with him does my poem live,
   And as the stream must follow the river's course,
     Where his thought goes I'm drawn, impelled to
       Follow the sure one through devious orbits.

Where to? where to? I hear you now here now there,
   You glorious one! And all round the earth it sounds.
     Where do you end? And what, what is it
       Lurks above clouds there, and what befalls me?

Day! Day! Above the tottering clouds, it's you
   I welcome back! My eyes are in flower for you.
     O light of youth! And joy, the same as
       Once! Yet more spiritual now you pour from

A holy chalice, pure golden source! And you,
   You verdant earth, our cradle of peace, and you,
     Ancestral house, and all you dear ones
       Met in the past, O draw near, assemble,

O come that yours, that yours be the joy, return
   And all receive the seeing man's blessing now!
     O take, that I may bear it, take this
       Life, the divine, from my heart too burdened.

THE POET'S COURAGE

Is not all that's alive close and akin to you,
   Does the Fate not herself keep you to serve her ends?
      Well, then, travel defenceless
         On through life, and fear nothing there!

All that happens there be welcome, be blessed to you,
   Be an adept in joy, or is there anything
      That could harm you there, heart, that
         Could offend you, where you must go?

For, as quiet near shores, or in the silvery
   Flood resounding afar, or over silent deep
      Water travels the flimsy
         Swimmer, likewise we love to be

Where around us there breathe, teem those alive, our kind,
   We, their poets; and glad, friendly to every man,
      Trusting all. And how else for
         Each of them could we sing his god?

Though the wave will at times, flattering, drag below
   One such brave man where, true, trusting he makes his
                        way,
      And the voice of that singer
         Now falls mute as the hall turns blue;

Glad he died there, and still lonely his groves lament
   Him whom most they had loved, lost, though with joy he
                       drowned;
      Often a virgin will hear his
         Kindly song in the distant boughs.

✻ 55

When at nightfall a man like him, of our kind, comes
   Past the place where he sank, many a thought he'll give
     To the site and the warning,
        Then in silence, more armed, walk on.

HOMECOMING

to his relatives

1

There in the alps a gleaming night still delays and,
                             composing
  Portents of gladness, the cloud covers a valley agape.
This way, that way roars and rushes the breeze of the
                             mountains,
  Teasing, sheer through the firs falls a bright beam, and is
                             lost.
Slowly it hurries and wars, this Chaos trembling with
                             pleasure,
  Young in appearance, but strong, celebrates here amid
                             rocks
Loving discord, and seethes, shakes in its bounds that are
                             timeless,
  For more bacchantically now morning approaches within.
For more endlessly there the year expands, and the holy
  Hours and the days in there more boldly are ordered and
                             mixed.
Yet the bird of thunder marks and observes the time, and
  High in the air, between peaks, hangs and calls out a new
                             day.
Now, deep inside, the small village also awakens and
                             fearless
  Looks at the summits around, long now familiar with
                             height;
Growth it foreknows, for already ancient torrents like
                             lightning
  Crash, and the ground below steams with the spray of
                             their fall.

Echo sounds all around and, measureless, tireless the
                                        workshop,
    Sending out gifts, is astir, active by day and by night.

2

Quiet, meanwhile, above, the silvery peaks lie aglitter,
    Full of roses up there, flushed with dawn's rays, lies the
                                        snow.
Even higher, beyond the light, does the pure, never clouded
    God have his dwelling, whom beams, holy, make glad
                                        with their play.
Silent, alone he dwells, and bright his countenance shines
                                        now,
    He, the æthereal one, seems kindly, disposed to give life,
Generate joys, with us men, as often when, knowing the
                                        measure,
    Knowing those who draw breath, hesitant, sparing the
                                        God
Sends well-allotted fortune both to the cities and houses,
    Showers to open the land, gentle, and you, brooding
                                        clouds,
You, then, most dearly loved breezes, followed by temperate
                                        springtime,
    And with a slow hand once more gladdens us mortals
                                        grown sad,
When he renews the seasons, he, the creative, and quickens,
    Moves once again those hearts weary and numb with old
                                        age,
Works on the lowest depths to open them up and to
                                        brighten
    All, as he loves to do; so now does life bud anew,
Beauty abounds, as before, and spirit is present, returned
                                        now,
    And a joyful zest urges furled wings to unfold.

3

Much I said to him; for whatever the poets may ponder,
  Sing, it mostly concerns either the angels or him.
Much I besought, on my country's behalf, lest unbidden one
                    day the
  Spirit should suddenly come, take us by storm
                    unprepared;
Much, too, for your sake to whom, though troubled now in
                    our country,
  Holy gratitude brings fugitives back with a smile,
Fellow Germans, for your sake! Meanwhile the lake gently
                    rocked me,
  Calmly the boatman sat, praising the weather, the breeze.
Out on the level lake one impulse of joy had enlivened
  All the sails, and at last, there in a new day's first hour
Brightening, the town unfurls, and safely conveyed from the
                    shadows
  Cast by the Alps, now the boat glides to its mooring and
                    rests.
Warm the shore is here, and valleys open in welcome,
  Pleasantly lit by paths, greenly allure me and gleam.
Gardens, forgathered, lie here and already the dew-laden
                    bud breaks
  And a bird's early song welcomes the traveller home.
All seems familiar; even the word or the nod caught in
                    passing
  Seems like a friend's, every face looks like a relative's face.

4

And no wonder! Your native country and soil you are
                    walking,
  What you seek, it is near, now comes to meet you

halfway.
Nor by mere chance like a son a wandering man now stands
gazing
Here by the wavelet-loud gate, looking for names to
convey
Love to you in his poem, Lindau, the favoured and happy!
Not the least of our land's many hospitable doors,
Urging men to go out allured by the promise of distance,
Go where the wonders are, go where that godlike wild
beast,
High up the Rhine blasts his reckless way to the plains of the
lowlands,
Where out of rocks at last bursts the lush valley's delight,
Wander in there, through the sunlit mountain range, making
for Como,
Or, as the day drifts on, drift on the wide open lake;
Yet, you door that are hallowed, me much more strongly
you urge to
Make for home where I know blossoming pathways and
lanes,
There to visit the fields and the Neckar's beautiful valleys,
And the woods, green leaves holy to me, where the oak
Does not disdain to consort with quiet birches and beeches,
Where amid mountains one place holds me, a captive
content.

5

There they too receive me. Voice of my town, of my mother!
How to your sound respond things that I learned long
ago!
Yet they are still themselves! More radiantly, almost, than
ever,
Dearest ones, in your eyes joy and the sun are alight.
Yes, it's all what it was. It thrives and grows ripe, but no
creature

Living and loving there ever abandons its faith.
But the best thing of all, the find that's been saved up
                              beneath the
Holy rainbow of peace, waits for the young and the old.
Like a fool I speak. In my joy. But tomorrow and later
  When we go outside, look at the living green field
Under the trees in blossom, on holidays due in the
                              springtime,
  Much of those things with you, dear ones, I'll speak and
                              I'll hope.
Much in the meantime I've heard of him, the great Father,
                              and long now
  I have kept silent about him who on summits renews
Wandering Time up above and governs the high mountain
                              ranges,
  Him who soon now will grant heavenly gifts and calls
                              forth
Song more effulgent, and sends us many good spirits. No
                              longer
  Wait now, preservers, the year's angels, O come now, and
                              you,

6

Angels, too, of our house, re-enter the veins of all life now,
  Gladdening all at once, let what is heavenly be shared!
Make us noble and new! Till nothing that's humanly good,
                              no
  Hour of the day without them, them the most joyful, or
                              such
Joy as now too is known when lovers return to each other,
  Passes, as fitting for them, hallowed as angels demand.
When we bless the meal, whose name may I speak, and
                              when late we
  Rest from the life of each day, tell me, to whom give my
                              thanks?

Him, the most High, should I name then? A god does not
                              love what's unseemly,
  Him to embrace and to hold our joy is too small.
Silence often behoves us: while the lips hesitate, wary of
                              speech?
Yet a lyre to each hour lends the right mode, the right music,
  And, it may be, delights heavenly ones who draw near.
This make ready, and almost nothing remains of the care
                              that
  Darkened our festive day, troubled the promise of joy.
Whether he like it or not, and often, a singer must harbour
  Cares like these in his soul; not, though, the wrong sort of
                              cares.

from THE DEATH OF EMPEDOCLES

Second version

Your movement hushed, you came into my stillness,
Deep in the gloomy hall you sought me out,
You kindly light; and not unhoped for came,
But from afar, at work above the earth,
Well I could hear you come again, bright Day!
And my familiars, you the quick and busy
Powers of the heights – now you are close to me
Once more, as once you were, the joyous,
Trees of my grove that neither stray nor falter!
You rested there and grew there well-contented
Since daily Heaven's own well-springs watered you
With light, and Aether on the flowering scattered
Sparks of pure life that fertilized their bloom.
O intimate Nature, close again to my eyes,
Do you still know your friend, the fondly loved,
Or never again will you acknowledge me,
The priest who brought you gifts of living song,
Offered it up like life-blood gladly shed?

Third version

You now I call upon across the fields,
Call down and in from the slow clouds, hot sunrays
Of noontide, you the most matured, so that
In you I'll recognise my new life's day.
For all is different now; and gone, dispelled,
My human grief! as though grown birdlike, graced
With pinions overnight, I feel so light
Up here, so well, and rich enough and glad
And glorious here I dwell where Father Etna
Tenders hospitably the fiery chalice
Filled to the brim with spirit, garlanded
With flowers that for himself he has reared up.

[...]

Yes, we live peacefully; and vastly here
The holy elements reveal themselves.
Ever the same, the untoiling joyously,
Surely and powerfully stir around us.
On its firm shores advances and reposes
The ancient sea, and the great mountains rise
With music of their springs, the green woods flow
And roar and rustle down from vale to vale.
And at the top light lingers, Aether stills
Our minds and the more secret of our longings.
Here we live peacefully.

HALF OF LIFE

With yellow pears hangs down
And full of wild roses
The land into the lake,
You loving swans,
And drunk with kisses
You dip your heads
Into water, the holy-and-sober.

But oh, where shall I find
When winter comes, the flowers, and where
The sunshine
And shade of the earth?
The walls loom
Speechless and cold, in the wind
Weathercocks clatter.

MNEMOSYNE

Third version

Ripe are, dipped in fire, cooked
The fruits and tried on the earth, and it is law,
Prophetic, that all must enter in
Like serpents, dreaming on
The mounds of heaven. And much
As on the shoulders a
Load of logs must be
Retained. But evil are
The paths, for crookedly
Like horses go the imprisoned
Elements and ancient laws
Of the earth. And always
There is a yearning that seeks the unbound. But much
Must be retained. And loyalty is needed.
Forward, however, and back we will
Not look. Be lulled and rocked as
On a swaying skiff of the sea.

   But how, my dear one? On the ground
Sunshine we see and the dry dust
And, a native sight, the shadows of forests, and on roof-
                             tops
There blossoms smoke, near ancient crests
Of the turrets, peaceable; for good indeed
When, contradicting, the soul
Has wounded one of the Heavenly, are the signs of day.
For snow, like lilies of the valley
By indicating where
The noble-minded is, shines brightly
On the green meadow

Of the Alps, half melted, where
Discoursing of the cross which once was placed
There on the wayside for the dead,
High up, in anger, distantly divining
A traveller walks
With the other, but what is this?

   Beside the fig tree
My Achilles has died and is lost to me,
And Ajax lies
Beside the grottoes of the sea,
Beside brooks that neighbour Scamandros.
Of a rushing noise in his temples once,
According to the changeless custom of
Unmoved Salamis, in foreign parts
Great Ajax died,
Not so Patroclus, dead in the King's own armour.
And many others died. But by Cithaeron there stood
Eleutherae, Mnemosyne's town. From her also
When God laid down his festive cloak, soon after did
The powers of Evening sever a lock of hair. For the heavenly,
                              when
Someone has failed to collect his soul, to spare it,
Are angry, for still he must; like him
Here mourning is at fault.

Friedrich Hölderlin

Friedrich Hölderlin

Susette Gonthard

NOTES ON THE POEMS

Please also refer to the Bibliography

An Diotima, To Diotima

The name Diotima comes from the priestess who taught Socrates about love in the *Symposium*. Friedrich Hölderlin eulogized Susette Gontard as Diotima in other poems, such as 'Diotima', 'To Her Genius' and 'Menon's Lament for Diotima'; she was the hero's beloved in his novel *Hyperion*.

Hyperions Schiksaalslied, Hyperion's Song of Fate

One of Friedrich Hölderlin's most popular poems. In his *Journals* André Gide wrote 'I plunge with rapture into Hölderlin's *Hyperion*, happy to understand it so well' (André Gide, *Journals 1889-1949*, ed. & tr. Justin O'Brien, Penguin, 1967, 419). In *Hyperion* Hölderlin spoke of inner strength:

> The secret power within you announces it, the power from which your eternal growth derives its strength. Let your blossom fall, your branches wither. You bear within you the germ of eternity. (in A. Stansfield, 47)

One of the climaxes of *Hyperion* is the pantheistic message:

Men drop from you like rotten fruit, oh, let them perish, and to your
root they shall return, and I, O Tree of Life, let me grow verdant again
with you and waft around your crests with all your burgeoning twigs!
Peaceful and closely akin for all of us grew out of the golden seed-grain.
(in M. Hamburger, 1970, 51)

Des Morgens, In the Morning

Written in 1799. In 'Des Morgens', Friedrich Hölderlin sends
out passionate lines to the sky, evocative incantations that poets
have written or spoken since time immemorial.

«*Geh unter, schöne sonne*», "Go down, then, lovely sun"

In "Geh unter, schöne Sonne", Friedrich Hölderlin combines a
number of elements: it begins as a hymn to his beloved god of
the sun, then moves on to tell of how the poet learned about
'godly, silent reverence' from his Diotima; it finishes with an
evocation of nature's splendour, and the re-connection of the poet
with nature once again. It is about refreshment, the re-
invigoration that nature/ love/ the sun/ the gods/ the beloved
can bring.

Die Liebe, Love

In 'Die Liebe', Friedrich Hölderlin expresses sentiments similar
to those from Rainer Maria Rilke's *Sonnets to Orpheus*, where
Rilke implores the reader to become more than s/he is. Hölderlin
apostrophizes 'Love', love as a God, the abstraction that was made
into a deity by the Greeks, so that the troubadours, a millennium
later, could write endless *cansos* and lovesongs addressed to
'Love', or 'Eros', or 'Cupid'. In Hölderlin's poesie, 'Love' is not
the 'Amor' of courtly love, but the God of pantheism, the spirit of
life itself, which, as with Rilke, the poet implores to grow and
grow.

Unter den Alpen Gesungen, Sung Beneath the Alps

Friedrich Hölderlin's only completed Sapphic ode. Hölderlin had crossed the Alps on foot in January, 1801, to take up another private tutorship.

Der Blinde Sänger, The Blind Singer

The Sophocles epigraph is from the *Ajax*, line 706. Friedrich Hölderlin translated Sophocles' *Oedipus Rex* and *Antigone*.

Dichtermuth, The Poet's Courage

In 'Dichtermuth', Friedrich Hölderlin recommends that poet go through life fearlessly, as well as defencelessly. As poets are so 'close and akin' to life, nothing can startle them or unsettle them.

Heimkunft, Homecoming

Ronald Peacock writes that it is 'but one expression of a constantly recurring theme: the coming of Day, in all its extended senses... the home-coming itself is the beginning of a new period in life... We are again at the origins of Hölderlin's poetry, his belief in life, in the potentiality of nature and man' (90-91).

from *Der Tod des Empedokles*, from *The Death of Empedocles*

'Hölderlin believed that only true humility could teach the poet to use the gift of speech in the right way at the right moment', writes L.S. Salzberger of *The Death of Empedocles*, adding, 'Empedokles has failed in this, and his punishment is that he is to be the mouthpiece of the gods no longer' (1952, 35).

The opening of the third version of *The Death of Empedocles* recalls some of Prospero's speeches, in *The Tempest*. Like Prospero, Empedocles has to re-align himself with his fundamental and inescapable humanity. He has to learn that his powers are limited. In *The Death of Empedocles* there are moments of serenity recalling Prospero on his Mediterranean island. It seems sometimes as if Friedrich Hölderlin were consciously evoking the imagery and language of William Shakespeare's play of resignation and maturity.

Hälfte des Lebens, Half of Life

Friedrich Hölderlin's sense of ecstasy is not that of the decadent slide into drugs and debauchery of certain strands of Romanticism (Samuel Taylor Coleridge with his opium, John Keats with his poppy-laden imagery). Hölderlin's sense of rapture is distinctly clear-headed. The phrase from 'Hälfte des Lebens' comes to mind: describing water, the poet calls it 'heilignüchterne' (holy-and-sober'). This describes Hölderlin's ecstatic outlook: blissful, holy, but also sober, clear. Not drunk or dissipated, not brought low by drugs, but pure, holy.

Mnemosyne, Mnemosyne

Mnemosyne was the mother of the Muses.

A NOTE ON FRIEDRICH HÖLDERLIN

by Jeremy Mark Robinson

Friedrich Hölderlin was born Johann Friedrich Hölderlin on March 20, 1770 in Lauffen, a Swabian town on the River Neckar. For Ronald Peacock, Hölderlin was the poet of 'radiant purity', 'the one whose name can be uttered only in the tone of veneration' (1973, 1). Much has been made of his relationship with his mother, and his dependence on her (his father died in 1772, when Hölderlin was an infant, and his step-father died in 1779).

Friedrich Hölderlin studied at the local grammar school until 1784; he was a boarder at the Lower Monastery School (in Denkendorf) and the Upper Monastery School (in Maulbronn). At Tübingen, a town that crops up many times in Hölderlin's biography, he studied for his inordination from 1788-93. His friends at Tübingen included Georg Wilhelm Friedrich Hegel, Rudolf Friedrich Heinrich von Magenau and Friedrich Wilhelm Joseph Schelling. As a student, Hölderlin read Friedrich Schiller's

Philosophische Briefe, F.H. Jakobi's *Über die Lehre des Spinoza in Briefen an Herrn Moses Mendelsohn*, Joseph Gottfried Herder, Tiberius Hemsterhuis, as well as the occultist Giordano Bruno. He was enamoured, like so many poets of the time, of the French Revolution. He wrote many poems at Tübingen, as well as student theses on the links between Solomon's proverbs and Hesiod's *Works and Days*, and on Greek art (*Die Geschichte der schönen Künste unter den Griechen*). Friedrich Gottlieb Klopstock (1724-1803) and Johann Christoph Friedrich von Schiller (1759-1805) were two of Hölderlin's poetic models at this time.

Hölderlin idolized Schiller excessively. He wrote in August, 1797 that he could not remain in proximity to Schiller: 'you excite me too much, when I am with you'.[1] Since he was young Hölderlin had worshipped Schiller, so when he met him at Jena, Hölderlin was over-awed. The adoration seemed to be one-sided, Schiller regarding Hölderlin as an eager, talented but 'rather helpless young fellow-Swabian' (ib., 21). The friendship with Schiller was crucial for Hölderlin; though he tried, he couldn't escape Schiller's influence over him. At times, writes E.M. Butler, it seemed as if Schiller were speaking through Hölderlin; Hölderlin seemed to have taken over Schiller's project as his own. At times, in Jena, Hölderlin was so taken over by Schiller's presence that he was hardly aware of other people in the room – even luminaries such as Johann Wolfgang von Goethe (1749-1832), the king of German literature. Hölderlin had not heard Schiller's introduction of Goethe when was visiting Schiller, and thus largely ignored the great man; 'but, had I known what I now know I should have grown deadly pale', Hölderlin said afterwards.[2]

This was the time when Friedrich Hölderlin was attempting to sustain himself financially by writing – and failing. 'Hölderlin was still fighting for freedom, for something within him, precious and sacred, untouchable, inviolable, of which he was dimly aware but passionately certain', wrote Agnes Stansfield (39). The irony is that, though Hölderlin kept trying to get Friedrich Schiller to acknowledge his own poetic talents, Schiller never recognized them. Johann Wolfgang von Goethe, too, did not or would not acknowledge Hölderlin's talent (Goethe also failed to recognize Heinrich Heine's creativity).

Friedrich Hölderlin did not take up the religious calling, the ministry, which his family (particularly his mother) had been expecting of him for years. Hölderlin refrained from telling his mother about his religious doubts. He knew his questioning would upset her. He informed her, though, that he had been studying philosophy. Benedict Spinoza's thought, he told her, seemed reasonable (A. Stansfield, 26). Instead, Hölderlin became a private tutor. Working for Charlotte von Kalb's son, at Waltershausen, Hölderlin wrote his novel *Hyperion* in 1793. After his time with Frau von Kalb, Hölderlin spoke of wanting to live by writing alone, 'to keep my body and my soul alive by my own works' (in A. Stansfield, 41), one of the primary desires of most writers. His patron and mentor in the 1790s was Friedrich Schiller.

At Jena Hölderlin met some of the key figures of German Romanticism – not only Schiller, but also Johann Wolfgang von Goethe, Georg Wilhelm Friedrich Hegel and Johann Gottlieb Fichte. A meeting at Friedrich Immanuel Niethammer's Jena house in May, 1795 included Fichte, Schiller, Novalis, Niethammer and Hölderlin. The record of what was said at this meeting of some of the great talents of German Romanticism is vague. Niethammer said they had talked about revelation, religion and philosophy – no surprises there.[3]

The chief love in Friedrich Hölderlin's life was Susette Borkenstein Gontard (1769-1802), the 'beautiful, cultured and noble' wife of a Frankfurt banker, J.F. Gontard.[4] Hölderlin taught Gontard's children. He did not tell his mother about Gontard – she would not have approved. He idealized Gontard: she became his Muse, the Diotima in his poetry. 'Schönes Leben! du lebst, wie die zarten Blüthen im Winter', Hölderlin wrote in 'To Diotima'.[5] Just as Novalis worshipped his beloved Sophie von Kühn as an embodiment of Sophia (Wisdom), a Goddess of transcendent philosophy, so Hölderlin apostrophized Susette Gontard as Diotima in poems such as 'Diotima', 'To Diotima', 'To Her Genius' and 'Menon's Lament for Diotima'. Diotima was the hero's beloved in Hölderlin's novel *Hyperion*. 'Shelley, and Hölderlin above all, with his own 'Diotima',' writes George Steiner, 'are inebriate with the sensuality of the psyche when it is possessed by love'.[6]

Many poems are addressed to Diotima, and she is the subject of many pieces. The exaltation of Diotima also enabled Friedrich Hölderlin to move away from Friedrich Schiller's huge influence, so that he could focus on something else. It was with his relationship with Susette Gontard that Hölderlin's poetry began to develop rapidly, achieving a depth and lyricism far beyond the early poems. Gontard, as Diotima, was crucial in this poetic development.

Friedrich Hölderlin's relationship with Gontard was relatively brief, however. They perhaps enjoyed a greater intimacy in 1796, when Gontard and her children left Frankfurt for Kassel to avoid the French army. In 1798, though, Gontard sent Hölderlin away after an altercation, or he left secretly, depending on which biography is consulted. Hölderlin escaped to nearby Homburg; the lovers kept in touch via letters and occasional secret meetings. Not many of Hölderlin's love letters have survived, but Susette Gontard's, which were published in 1921, are, according to L.S. Salzberger, 'among the finest love letters in literature' (25).

Publicly separated, the lovers contrived to meet in secret, meeting once a month, though their times together at each encounter were short, and Susette Gontard did not have long to live. Gontard arranged for a meeting on the first Thursday of each month at the theatre. Gontard asked Friedrich Hölderlin to walk beneath her window, so she could see how he was. 'O! my heart! how I thank you. You are there... Ah, I have surely not seen you for the last time', she wrote to him of one of her Thursday glimpses of him. 'Almost every letter reveals how entirely her life had become dependent on his', commented J.B. Leishman.[7] In her letters she said she was trying 'to save the best and most beautiful thing in the world from destruction' (ib., 219). 'If it must be that we are to be sacrifices of Fate,' Gontard wrote to Hölderlin,

> then promise me to make yourself free of me and to live as will make you happy, as will enable you to fulfil your duties on this earth according to your knowledge of them, and let my image be no hindrance. Only this promise can give me peace and contentment. Such love as I bear you no one will ever know, nor will you ever love again as you loved me. (in A. Stansfield, 83)

The separation from Susette Gontard deeply affected Friedrich Hölderlin. After this time, his poetry became increasingly 'tragic'. Significantly, the protagonist in Hölderlin's play *The Death of Empedocles* is separated from everything he loves, including the gods and nature, and the cosmos itself. Hölderlin did not complete *The Death of Empedocles*, despite taking it through three versions. Of other projects of the late 1790s, such as *The Death of Socrates* and a tragedy (*Agis*), nothing remains. For some critics, *Der Tod des Empedokles* is 'almost beyond admiration'; it transcends Johann Wolfgang von Goethe's *Faust* and Percy Bysshe Shelley's *Prometheus Unbound,* and, according to E.M. Butler,

> Only the *Prometheus* of Aeschylus can be compared to it for sublimity of thought and of tragic conception.[8]

The philosopher Empedocles (*ca.* 490-430 B.C.) was one of the great minds of the Classical Greek era. He was given to statements which veered into the realms of magic. Of the transmigration of the soul, he said (in fragment 117): 'already I have once been a boy and a girl, a fish and a bird and a dumb sea fish'.[9] Empedocles also wrote: 'I go about among you all an immortal god, mortal no more, honoured as is my due and crowned with garlands and verdant wreaths' (ib., 354).

The Death of Empedocles is not a particularly 'dramatic' play, more poetic than traditional theatrical drama. The hero is the centre of the piece – the other characters are minor. The tragedy of *Der Tod des Empedokles* pivots around the inescapable humanity of the hero, that is, the conflict between the human and the divine, which's one of Friedrich Hölderlin's great themes. The tragedy for Empedocles is to realize, prophet and shaman though he is, he is not one of the gods.

After the separation from Susette Gontard in September, 1798, Friedrich Hölderlin went to Homburg vor der Höhe, until 1800. Once a month Hölderlin would meet Gontard: they swapped letters. Unfortunately, Gontard destroyed Hölderlin's letters, but he kept hers hidden away for forty years. 'It is your duty,' Gontard told him in a letter, 'to give to the world in a higher form that which appears to you transfigured' (A. Stansfield, 83).

At Homburg Friedrich Hölderlin was introduced to the Landgrave of Homburg. The latter's daughter, Princess Auguste, became an ardent admirer of Hölderlin's poetry, and Hölderlin dedicated a number of works to her (including his translations of *Antigone* and *Oedipus Rex*, and his last book publications). The Homburg circle included Georg Wilhelm Friedrich Hegel, Johann Gottfried Ebel, the poet Siegfried Schmid, the playwright Ulrich Böhlendorff, and Isaak von Sinclair, one of Hölderlin's most devoted friends, from his time in Jena. Sinclair helped Hölderlin later, when he began to decline mentally.

In 1799, Friedrich Hölderlin planned to launch a magazine (called *Iduna*, after the German Goddess of rebirth). Hölderlin's journal project foundered, though, when there was a poor response from potential contributors (Hölderlin had asked Friedrich Schelling, Karl Philipp Conz, Wilhelm Heinse, Ludwig Neuffer, Johann Wolfgang von Goethe and of course Friedrich Schiller for contributions). *Iduna* was to have included essays by Hölderlin on Greek drama, epic and lyric poetry, extracts from *The Death of Empedocles*, some Pindar translations; also pieces on Homer, *Prometheus, Antigone, Oedipus*, Horace's odes, the *Nouvelle Héloïse, Antony and Cleopatra, Macbeth* and Julius Caesar, an *Ossian* translation, among other items. Unfortunately, contributors such as Schelling were reluctant to support the *Iduna* journal, while others such as Schiller discouraged Hölderlin.

Friedrich Hölderlin felt increasingly lonely from 1799 onwards, a societal outsider. He was frustrated in finding a way of being a self-sufficient writer, and piquantly felt the separation from his lover, Gontard. The contacts with the greats of German Romanticism (Goethe, Schiller, Novalis, Hegel) did not satisfy his ambitions. Around 1799 and 1800 there were visits to various places in Germany: to Stuttgart as Christian Landauer's guest; to his home in Nürtingen; after Christmas, to Hauptwyl in Switzerland. Hölderlin usually walked between these places. He walked, for example, to Hauptwyl, crossing the Alps in January. Poems of this time ('Sung beneath the Alps' and 'Homecoming', both included here) depict snowy Alpine scenes. The journey to his last engagement as a private tutor, to Bordeaux in January, 1802, took over a month on foot (Hölderlin armed himself with pistols for the hazardous journey). Not much is known about Hölderlin's time in Bordeaux. There are rumours about his life there, and intimations of his oncoming mental disturbance.

It was after the return journey from Bordeaux that Friedrich Hölderlin suffered his 'madness'. Susette Gontard was ill – she died on June 22, 1802, from German measles caught from her children. The news of her death, communicated to him by a letter to Landauer from Isaak von Sinclair (written on June 30, 1802), may have contributed to his psychic decline. Certainly her death was a massive loss – she was his Muse, after all, and he valued poetry above nearly everything. 'Hölderlin reached the summit of poetry before she died, and he achieved it largely through her', remarked E.M. Butler (1935, 219). Sinclair offered Hölderlin money and a place to stay, which Hölderlin did not take up. Hölderlin was a sensitive, moody personality, who experienced extremes of emotion. After the breakdown, back in Nürtingen in July, 1802, he was haggard, withdrawn, given to rages and silences and strange utterances. His mother looked after him until

September, 1802, when he was well enough to visit Sinclair.

Charlotte von Kalb and Isaak von Sinclair organized the publication of Friedrich Hölderlin's translations of Sophocles. At this time Hölderlin took long walks and returned too tired to work at his desk. Friedrich Schiller found the Sophocles translations laughable. It might have upset Hölderlin, had he known about Schiller's reaction. But by this time, mid-1804, Hölderlin's illness was increasing, despite Sinclair writing to his mother to say he was more balanced. The doctor who examined Hölderlin said he was hypochondriacal. He suffered from bouts of nervous exhaustion and from colic when irritated.

In August, 1806 Friedrich Hölderlin could no longer stay at Homburg. Hölderlin was taken by force to the Autenrieth mental clinic in Tübingen. Here the regime included immersion in cold water in a cage, strait jackets, drugs (belladonna, digitalis), and the Autenrieth mask, put on to stop patients screaming.

Friedrich Hölderlin was rescued from this hell in the mental home by Ernst Zimmer, a carpenter, who took Hölderlin in 1807 to his house in Tübingen beside the River Neckar. Here, in a small room in Zimmer's 'tower', Hölderlin spent the rest of life (36 years), until his death on June 7, 1843, aged 73.

Friedrich Hölderlin's biography contains a huge gap of years, about which little is known. In one of the standard studies of Hölderlin (Ronald Peacock's *Hölderlin*), the chronology of the poet's life is printed like this:

1804 Translations of Sophocles published by Wilmans.
     Sinclair procures for Hölderlin position of librarian to Landgraf von Hessen-Homburg.
1805 Continued deterioration in health; dementia praecox (catatonic), with short periods of lucidity.
1806 Sinclair takes him to a private clinic in Tübingen.
1807 Lodged with the carpenter Zimmer.
1843 Death on 7 June.[10]

At Zimmer's house, Friedrich Hölderlin would go on long

walks and put stones in his pockets. He picked flowers and then destroyed them. He played the flute. He sang. He played one melody on a piano for hours.

Much has been written about Friedrich Hölderlin's 'madness', including the age-old question: is the poetry written during the 'madness' as good or valid as the work made in 'sanity'? Similar accusations are made of Vincent van Gogh, some of whose best works were made in states approaching 'mental instability'. The same arguments are levelled at artists taking drugs. However, Hölderlin could hardly have written such lucid, subtle, and radiant hymns and poems without periods of intense concentration.[11]

Ernst Zimmer reckoned that Friedrich Hölderlin had 'too much in him' and it 'cracked his mind'. Certainly, from even a cursory glance at his biography, Hölderlin comes across as a determined and yearning soul. The failure of the magazine project due to lack of interest is disheartening, but is a sign of a general trend in Hölderlin's life where he felt distanced from society and social contact. The separation from Susette Gontard is more serious: here Hölderlin's feelings of ineffectuality must have been greater, for he could not lay claim to Gontard. He was always the outsider in the Gontard household, where his employer was master.

Ernst Meister wonders if Friedrich Hölderlin let himself become mad, to make up for the 'ordinary' life that everyday people lead, 'the provincial or parochial life, as it were, in the island's interior, against which the whole being surges and breaks' (1989). E.M. Butler reckons that Hölderlin's instability arose from having to choose between his beloved Greek gods and Christ. 'His spirit, when called upon to renounce the dream by which it lived, renounced the dream and died' (1935, 238). It's a pity, perhaps, that Hölderlin did not write more during the years after the break in the middle of his life, but I think Michael Hamburger has it right when he says in his introduction to the poems:

Yet within a mere decade Hölderlin produced a poetic work so various, so rich in potentialities and possibilities for the 'future ages' in which he placed his hope, that regrets about it are out of place, as well as futile. Even his personal catastrophe is one that he foresaw at the start of that decade, willing to take the risk and pay the price; and, mad or not, even the verses he wrote in his decline, relapsing into generality and abstraction, can move us with faint echoes of his epiphanies, his verbal and visionary thunderclaps. (F. Hölderlin, 1994, xlii)

Friedrich Hölderlin's decline into mental illness is disturbing to contemplate. E.M. Butler speaks of 'this gruesome wreck of one of the greatest poets in the world' (1935, 238). It certainly is an amazing loss. But perhaps Hölderlin was burnt out anyway, in the way that Robert Graves speaks of most poets who burn bright while young then dry up and do something else. It seems as if it would have been difficult for Hölderlin to keep up the intensity and quality of his hymns and odes. On the other hand, poetry seems to flow effortlessly and profusely from him: perhaps, without madness, he could have continued to produce fluid, lyrical poetry.

It is sad to think of Friedrich Hölderlin becoming 'Scardanelli' or 'Killalusimeno': in his mental illness, he would not see himself as Hölderlin, but as the babbling figure of Scardanelli. Children in Tübingen were afraid of him, while students laughed at him. He apparently told a visitor who had over-stayed their welcome 'I am the Lord God', and showed him the door. In his later decline he forgot who he was. He spoke sometimes in 'an unintelligible mixture of German, Latin and Greek'.[12] He could be pacified by having Homer read to him. Wilhelm Waiblinger met Hölderlin in 1822 when the poet was still coherent. However, his three subjects of conversation were Oedipus, the Greeks, and suffering. Later, topics of conversation such as Greece, Frankfurt, Diotima and his poetry could not be mentioned. On one occasion Hölderlin screamed that Diotima had borne him many sons and was now insane. Hölderlin had been ill from time to time but had usually recovered swiftly. On the night of his death, June 6, 1843, he fell ill and sat for a long while by the open window for relief. Then he

lay down in bed, his hands folded as if he was praying. He died
at dawn.

※

Friedrich Hölderlin's poetry is not soft and gentle: it has more
than a few thunder storms and flashes of lightning, like much of
Romantic poetry. The atmospheres of the snowy Alps, the winds
of a mythic, remembered Greece (which he never visited), and
the wild woods of ancient Germany form the sensual foundation
of his poetry. The series of hymns and odes of the 1790s and early
1800s, the era of *Hyperion* and Hölderlin's Hellenic enthusiasm,
are extraordinary: 'Ermunterung' ('Exhortation'), 'Der Nekar'
('The Neckar'), 'An die Deutschen' ('To the Germans'), 'Gesang
des Deutschen' ('The German's Song'), 'Dichterberuf' ('The Poet's
Vocation'), 'Rükkehr in die Heimath' ('Return to the Homeland'),
and the poems in this book: 'Unter den Alpen Gesungen' ('Sung
Beneath the Alps'), 'Ihre Genesung' ('Her Recovery'), 'Geh
Unter, Schöne Sonne' ('Go down, then, lovely sun'), 'Palinode'
and 'Hyperions Schiksaalslied' ('Hyperion's Song of Fate'). Many
of the odes and hymns are energetic invocations to the gods (such
as Vulcan), to the ancient Greeks or modern day Germans, to
nature, or Mother Earth, or notions such as Peace, Hope, the
Homeland and Love, those personifications which require a
capital letter.

Many of the odes and hymns open with a passionate invocation
to the subject of the poem. Here are some examples:

• 'Palinode' begins with the poet calling to Earth: 'Why, Earth,
around me glimmer your friendly leaves?' (1994, 89);
• 'You holy heart of people, my father-land', the poet cries in
'The German's Song' (105);
• 'You gentle breezes, heralds of Italy', the poet sighs in
'Return to the Homeland' (155);
• 'You golden day, speed on to the peaks of heaven!' he intones
in 'In the Morning' (79);
• 'Vulcan' opens with an invocation to the fiery spirit thus:

'[y]ou come now, friendly spirit of fire' (201);
- 'The Gods' opens with '[y]ou silent Aether' (133);
- and one of the key Hölderlin poems, 'Hyperion's Song of Fate', opens breathlessly with:

You walk above in the light,
Weightless tread a soft floor, blessed genii! (65)

A few pieces, particularly the ones addressed to the sun or to light, have openings which ask the question, 'where are you now?': 'Where are you, youthful herald...?' the poet asks in 'The Blind Singer' (189).

Where are you, thought-infusing, which at this time
Must always move beside me, where are you, light?

the poet asks in 'Chiron' (193). And in 'To the Sun-God' the poet bemoans

Where are you? Dazzled, drunken my soul grows faint
And dark with so much gladness (45)

Friedrich Hölderlin believed in the notion of the poet as shaman, a *sacer vates* or *poeta theologus*, a prophet, the high priest of people, more William Blake than William Wordsworth.[13] Hölderlin related the *sacer vates* to poets such as Pierre de Ronsard, Sir Philip Sidney, Mario Girolamo Vida, John Milton, Friedrich Gottlieb Klopstock and Torquato Tasso (ib., 11). As he wrote in 'An die Deutschen' ('To the Germans'): 'sweet it is to divine, but an affliction too' (1994, 117). The early, idealistic Hölderlin saw the world in largely visionary terms; for him, history was a 'single long chain of divine manifestations', and writers such as Plato, Pindar, Klopstock and the psalmists were the interpreters of these visions (ib., 15). Hölderlin also wrote of the poet as a hero, someone potentially titanic, whom Hölderlin compared to Achilles and Hercules. On the one hand, Hölderlin exalted the power and stature of the hero figure; on the other hand, he recognized that humility was crucial. 'Hyperion's Song of Fate' is one of the best examples of Hölderlin's lyricism, his Orphic/ shamanic voice, his Hellenism, and his triumphant use of the hymn or ode form.

In a letter to Ulrich Böhlendorff of December, 1802, Friedrich Hölderlin wrote 'as it has been said of heroes, I may say that Apollo has struck me' (in L. Salzberger, 39-40). Some critics interpreted the line 'Apollo has struck me' as indicating sunstroke. The phrase expresses much of Hölderlin's outlook: the violence of the image is typical of Hölderlin's extreme emotions. He does not say 'melted softly in me', but 'struck me'. It is not the deity that is important – it might be Apollo, Zeus, Dionysius or Christ – but the force of the mystical influence. There is a feeling in Hölderlin's poetry that he is 'driven', and usually a sense, as with Friedrich Nietzsche, that he is being driven by a god (or the gods). In 1798 Hölderlin spoke of being haunted by an 'evil dæmon'. *Denn es waltet ein Gott in uns* ('for within us a god commands') describes accurately the sense of being energized from within that is found in the work of Hölderlin and Nietzsche (and also in poets such as John Keats, Arthur Rimbaud and Comte de Lautréamont). Rimbaud had his 'Genie', which appeared in *Illuminations*, Keats and Percy Shelley had various gods radiating through their verses (usually Pan or Apollo, or the gods of the wind, the clouds and thunder storms). Hölderlin's *Gott in uns* erupted into German poetry again in the figure of Rainer Maria Rilke's Angel in his *Duino Elegies* cycle.

Friedrich Hölderlin is the sort of poet that sees gods every-where: his poetry is populated by heroes, gods and shamans; there is the Father or God; there are gods of the sun, the wind, the sky, the earth; there are the gods of Olympus; there is Christ; there are the prophets, patriarchs, apostles and disciples of the *Bible*; there are Greek Titans, heroes and philosophers; and there are the heroes of the late 18th century: Napoleon Bonaparte, whom Hölderlin admired, Jean-Jacques Rousseau, and figures such as Martin Luther, Christopher Columbus, and the German emperor Henry IV.

Friedrich Hölderlin is a 'poet's poet', in the sense that he creates 'pure poetry', poetry which does not require footnotes or explications, poetry which comes from individual feeling and thought, poetry which, though it is a product of its time and fashion, as all art is, strikes out of its own, carving its own niche in the cultural fabric of the West, poetry which builds on pure lyricism, poetry which, despite his later madness, remains passionate and authentic, imbued with the authenticity of the artist creating at the height of his powers. Hölderlin's free rhythms were 'so easy and poised, the pattern so subtle, that the art is unobtrusive', wrote Ronald Peacock (156). He was humble in discussing his own work. There can be little argument now that Friedrich Hölderlin is one of the very greatest of all poets of any era.

Notes

Please also refer to the Bibliography

1. F. Hölderlin, quoted in L. Salzberger, 1952, 22.
2. F. Hölderlin, quoted in A. Stansfield, 40.
3. F. Niethammer, quoted in *Novalis Schriften,* 4, 588. On the Jena meetings, see E. Behler, 1993, 14-15; Jochen Hörisch: ""Seinis gut": Ein Jenaer Geistergesprächvom Mair 1795 im Hause Niethammer mit Fichte, Hölderlin und Hardenburg", in *Athenaeum: Jahrbuch für Romantik,* E. Behler, 1991, 279-282.
4. L. Salzberger, 1952, 25.
5. 'Beautiful being, you live as do delicate blossoms in winter' (1994, 6-7).
6. George Steiner: "Two Suppers", in 1995, 409.
7. J.B. Leishman, in F. Hölderlin, 1954, 29.
8. E.M. Butler, 1935, 224.
9. Empedocles, in *The Presocratic Philosophers*, tr. G.S. Kirk & J.E. Raven, Cambridge University Press, 1957.
10. R. Peacock, 1973, 172.
11. C. Bowra, 1955, 132.
12. E.M. Butler, 1935, 237.
13. See L. Salzberger, 1952, 8-12.

Select Bibliography

Friedrich Hölderlin

Hölderlin Sämtliche Werke, Große Stuttgarter Ausgabe, Stuttgart, 1943-77
Die Friedensfeier, ed. W. Binder & A. Kelletat, Tübingen, 1959
Hölderlin Folioheft, ed. D.E. Sattler & E.E. George, Frankfurt, 1986
Poems and Fragments, tr. M. Hamburger, Routledge, 1966
Poems and Fragments, tr. M. Hamburger, Cambridge University Press, 1980
Poems and Fragments, tr. M. Hamburger, Anvil Press, 1994
Selected Poems and Fragments, tr. M. Hamburger, Penguin, 1998
Hymns and Fragments, tr. R. Siebruth, Princeton University Press, 1984
Selected Verse, tr. M. Hamburger, Anvil Press, 1985
Selected Poems, tr. D. Constantine, Bloodaxe, 1996
Selected Poems [with Eduard Möricke], tr. C. Middleton, University of Chicago Press, 1972
What I Own: Versions of Hölderlin and Mandelstham [with Osip Mandelstham], Carcanet, 1998
Selected Poems, tr. J.B. Leishman, Hogarth Press, 1954
Complete Works, ed. N. von Hellingrath *et al*, Berlin, 1923
Essays and Letters on Theory, State University of New York Press, Albany, 1987
Hyperion, tr. W.R. Trask, Signet, New York, 1963
Hyperion and Selected Poems, ed. E.L. Santer, Continuum, 1992
Hölderlin's Madness, tr. D. Gascoyne, London, 1938

Others

E. Behler. *Confrontations: Derrida/ Heidegger/ Nietzsche*, Stanford University Press, Stanford, 1991

—. *German Romantic Literary Theory*, Cambridge University Press, 1993

T. Bahti. *Ends of the Lyric: Direction and Consequence in Western Poetry*, John Hopkins University Press, Baltimore, 1996

—. *et al*, eds. *Athenaeum: Jahrbuch für Romantik*, 1991, vol. 1

M.B. Benn. *Hölderlin and Pindar*, The Hague, 1962

E. Benz. *The Mystical Sources of German Romantic Philosophy*, tr. B. Reynolds & E. Paul, Pickwick, Allison Park, 1983

P. Bertaux. *Hölderlin; Essai de biographie intérieure*, Paris, 1936

—. *Le lyrisme mythique de Hölderlin*, Paris, 1936

P. Böckman. *Hölderlin und seine Götter*, Munich, 1931

C.M. Bowra. *Inspiration and Poetry*, Macmillan, 1955

E.M. Butler. *The Tyranny of Greece Over Germany*, Cambridge University Press, 1935

D. Constantine. *The Significance of Locality in the Poetry of Friedrich Hölderlin*, Modern Humanities Research Association, 1979

—. *Early Greek Travellers and the Hellenic Ideal*, Cambridge University Press, 1984

—. *Hölderlin*, Oxford University Press, 1988

S. Corngold. *Complex Pleasures: Forms of Feeling in German Literature*, Cambridge University Press, 1998

A. Del Caro. *Hölderlin: The Poetics of Being*, Wayne State University Press, 1991

P. de Man. "Les exégèses de Hölderlin par Martin Heidegger", *Critique*, 100, 1955

—. *Blindness and Insight*, University of Minnesota Press, Minneapolis, 1983

H. Eichner, ed. *'Romantic' and Its Cognates: The European History of a Word*, University of Toronto Press, 1972

A. Fioretos, ed. *The Solid Letter: Readings of Friedrich Hölderlin*, Stanford University Press, 1999

E. Förster, ed. *The Course of Remembrance and Other Essays on Hölderlin*, Cambridge University Press, 1997

H.-J. Frey. *Studies in Poetic Discourse: Mallarmé, Baudelaire, Rimbaud, Hölderlin*, tr. W. Whobrey, Cambridge University Press, 1996

S. Frierichsmeyer. *The Androgyne in Early German Romanticism: Friedrich Schlegel, Novalis and the Metaphysics of Love*, Bern, New York, 1983

M. Froment-Meurice. *Solitudes: From Rimbaud to Heidegger*, State University of New York Press, 1995

M. Hamburger. *Reason and Energy: Studies in German Literature*, Weidenfeld & Nicolson, 1970

—. *Testimonies: Selected Shorter Prose, 1950-1987*, Carcanet, 1989

—. *Collected Poems, 1941-1994*, Anvil Press Poetry, 1995

—. *The Truth of Poetry*, Anvil Press Poetry, 1996

A. Häny. *Hölderlin's Titanenmythos*, Zurich, 1948

M. Heidegger. *Erläuterungen zu Hölderlin Dichtung*, Frankfurt, 1951

—. *Approche de Hölderlin*, Gallimard, Paris, 1973

D. Heinrich. *Course of Remembrance*, ed. E. Förster, Harvard University Press, 1994

G.T. Hughes. *Romantic German Literature*, Edward Arnold, 1979

L. Kempter. *Hölderlin und die Mythologie*, Zurich, 1929

D.F. Krell. "Nietzsche Hölderlin Empedocles", *Graduate Faculty Philosophy Journal*, 15, 2, 1991

—. *Lunar Voices: Of Tragedy, Poetry, Fiction, and Thought*, Chicago University Press, 1995

—. *The Recalcitrant Art: Diotima's Letters to Hölderlin and Related Missives*, State University of New York Press, Albany, 2000

A. Kuzniar. *Delayed Endings: Nonclosure in Novalis and Hölderlin*, University of Georgia Press, Athens, 1987

J. Laplanche. *Hölderlin et la Question du Père*, Paris, 1961

E. Lehmann. *Hölderlins Lyrik*, Munich, 1922

G. Lemout. *The Poet as Thinker: Hölderlin in France*, Camden House, 1994

E.C. Mason. *Hölderlin and Goethe*, P. Lang, 1975

E. Meister. *Prosa, 1931 bis 1979*, Heidelberg, 1989

C. Middleton. *The Poet's Vocation: Letters of Hölderlin, Rimbaud and Hart Crane*, Austin, Texas, c. 1967

M. Montgomery. *Friedrich Hölderlin and the German Neo-Hellenic Movement*, London, 1923

E. Muir. "Hölderlin's *Patmos*", *The European Quarterly*, 1, 4, February, 1935

R. Nägele. *Text, Gesichte und Subjektivität in Hölderlins Dichtung*, Metzler, Stuttgart, 1985

K.J. Obenauer. *Hölderlin-Novalis*, Jena, 1925

Ogden. *Problems of Christ in the Work of Friedrich Hölderlin*, Modern Humanities Research Association, 1991

R. Peacock. *Hölderlin*, Methuen, 1973

A. Pellegrini. *Friedrich Hölderlin*, Walter de Gruter, Berlin, 1965

Quarterly Review of Literature, Hölderlin issue, X, 1/2, 1959

Roy. *Friedrich Hölderlin in the Context of Wurttemberg*, Rodopi B.V. Editions, 1994

L.S. Salzberger. *Hölderlin*, Cambridge University Press, 1952

E.L. Santer. *Friedrich Hölderlin: Narrative Vigilance and the Poetic Imagination*, New Brunswick, 1986

J. Schmidt. "Der Begriff des Zorns in Hölderlin Spätwerk", *Hölderlin-Jahrbuch*, 15, 1967

—. *Hölderlins letzte Hymnen*, Mohr, Tübingen, 1970

—. "Sobria ebrietatis: Hölderlins 'Hälfte des Lebens'", *Hölderlin-Jahrbuch*, 23, 1982

A. Seyhan. *Representation and its Discontents: The Critical Legacy of German Romanticism*, University of California Press, Berkeley, 1992

E. Sewell. *The Orphic Voice: Poetry and Natural History*, Routledge, 1961

R.C. Shelton. *Young Hölderlin*, P. Lang, 1973

D. Simpson *et al*, eds. *German Aesthetic and Literary Criticism*, Cambridge University Press, 3 vols, 1984-85

E.L. Stahl. *Hölderlin's Symbolism*, Oxford University Press, 1945

A. Stansfield. *Hölderlin*, Manchester University Press, 1944

G. Steiner. *No Passion Spent*, Faber, 1995

P. Szondi. *Hölderlin-Studien*, Insel, Frankfurt, 1967

—. "Der andere Pfeil: Zur Enstehungsgesichte des hymnischen Spätstils", *Hölderlin-Studien*, Suhrkamp, Frankfurt, 1970

—. *Einführung in die literarishe Hermeneutik*, eds. J. Bollack & H. Stierlin, Suhrkamp, Frankfurt, 1975

R. Taylor. *The Romantic Tradition in Germany*, Methuen, 1970

R. Ungar. *Hölderlin's Major Poetry*, Indiana University Press, Bloomington, 1975

—. *Friedrich Hölderlin*, Twayne, 1984

A. Warminksi. *Readings in Interpretation: Hölderlin, Hegel, Heidegger*, University of Minnesota Press, Minneapolis, 1987

K. Wheeler, ed. *German Aesthetic and Literary Criticism, The Romantic Ironists and Goethe*, Cambridge University Press, 1984

CRESCENT MOON PUBLISHING

ARTS, PAINTING, SCULPTURE

The Art of Andy Goldsworthy: Complete Works
Andy Goldsworthy: Touching Nature
Andy Goldsworthy in Close-Up
Andy Goldsworthy: Pocket Guide
Andy Goldsworthy In America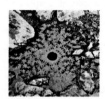
Land Art: A Complete Guide
The Art of Richard Long: Complete Works
Richard Long: Pocket Guide
Land Art In the UK
Land Art in Close-Up
Land Art In the U.S.A.
Land Art: Pocket Guide
Installation Art in Close-Up
Minimal Art and Artists In the 1960s and After
Colourfield Painting
Land Art DVD, TV documentary
Andy Goldsworthy DVD, TV documentary
The Erotic Object: Sexuality in Sculpture From Prehistory to the Present Day
Sex in Art: Pornography and Pleasure in Painting and Sculpture
Postwar Art
Sacred Gardens: The Garden in Myth, Religion and Art
Glorification: Religious Abstraction in Renaissance and 20th Century Art
Early Netherlandish Painting
Leonardo da Vinci
Piero della Francesca
Giovanni Bellini
Fra Angelico: Art and Religion in the Renaissance
Mark Rothko: The Art of Transcendence
Frank Stella: American Abstract Artist
Jasper Johns
Brice Marden
Alison Wilding: The Embrace of Sculpture
Vincent van Gogh: Visionary Landscapes
Eric Gill: Nuptials of God
Constantin Brancusi: Sculpting the Essence of Things
Max Beckmann
Caravaggio
Gustave Moreau
Egon Schiele: Sex and Death In Purple Stockings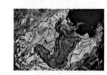
Delizioso Fotografico Fervore: Works In Process 1
Sacro Cuore: Works In Process 2
The Light Eternal: J.M.W. Turner
The Madonna Glorified: Karen Arthurs

LITERATURE

J.R.R. Tolkien: The Books, The Films, The Whole Cultural Phenomenon
J.R.R. Tolkien: Pocket Guide
Tolkien's Heroic Quest
The *Earthsea* Books of Ursula Le Guin
Beauties, Beasts and Enchantment: Classic French Fairy Tales
German Popular Tales by the Brothers Grimm
Philip Ullman and *His Dark Materials*
Sexing Hardy: Thomas Hardy and Feminism
Thomas Hardy's *Tess of the d'Urbervilles*
Thomas Hardy's *Jude the Obscure*
Thomas Hardy: The Tragic Novels
Love and Tragedy: Thomas Hardy
The Poetry of Landscape in Hardy
Wessex Revisited: Thomas Hardy and John Cowper Powys
Wolfgang Iser: Essays and Interviews
Petrarch, Dante and the Troubadours
Maurice Sendak and the Art of Children's Book Illustration
Andrea Dworkin
Cixous, Irigaray, Kristeva: The *Jouissance* of French Feminism
Julia Kristeva: Art, Love, Melancholy, Philosophy, Semiotics and Psychoanalysis
Hélene Cixous I Love You: The *Jouissance* of Writing
Luce Irigaray: Lips, Kissing, and the Politics of Sexual Difference
Peter Redgrove: Here Comes the Flood
Peter Redgrove: Sex-Magic-Poetry-Cornwall
Lawrence Durrell: Between Love and Death, East and West
Love, Culture & Poetry: Lawrence Durrell
Cavafy: Anatomy of a Soul
German Romantic Poetry: Goethe, Novalis, Heine, Hölderlin
Feminism and Shakespeare
Shakespeare: Love, Poetry & Magic
The Passion of D.H. Lawrence
D.H. Lawrence: Symbolic Landscapes
D.H. Lawrence: Infinite Sensual Violence
Rimbaud: Arthur Rimbaud and the Magic of Poetry
The Ecstasies of John Cowper Powys
Sensualism and Mythology: The Wessex Novels of John Cowper Powys
Amorous Life: John Cowper Powys and the Manifestation of Affectivity (H.W. Fawkner)
Postmodern Powys: New Essays on John Cowper Powys (Joe Boulter)
Rethinking Powys: Critical Essays on John Cowper Powys
Paul Bowles & Bernardo Bertolucci
Rainer Maria Rilke
Joseph Conrad: *Heart of Darkness*
In the Dim Void: Samuel Beckett
Samuel Beckett Goes into the Silence
André Gide: Fiction and Fervour
Jackie Collins and the Blockbuster Novel
Blinded By Her Light: The Love-Poetry of Robert Graves
The Passion of Colours: Travels In Mediterranean Lands
Poetic Forms

POETRY

Ursula Le Guin: Walking In Cornwall
Peter Redgrove: Here Comes The Flood
Peter Redgrove: Sex-Magic-Poetry-Cornwall
Dante: Selections From the *Vita Nuova*
Petrarch, Dante and the Troubadours
William Shakespeare: *The Sonnets*
William Shakespeare: Complete Poems
Blinded By Her Light: The Love-Poetry of Robert Graves
Emily Dickinson: Selected Poems
Emily Brontë: Poems
Thomas Hardy: Selected Poems
Percy Bysshe Shelley: Poems
John Keats: Selected Poems
D.H. Lawrence: Selected Poems
Edmund Spenser: Poems
Edmund Spenser: *Amoretti*
John Donne: Poems
Henry Vaughan: Poems
Sir Thomas Wyatt: Poems
Robert Herrick: Selected Poems
Rilke: Space, Essence and Angels in the Poetry of Rainer Maria Rilke
Rainer Maria Rilke: Selected Poems
Friedrich Hölderlin: Selected Poems
Arseny Tarkovsky: Selected Poems
Novalis: *Hymns To the Night*
Paul Verlaine: Selected Poems
Arthur Rimbaud: Selected Poems
Arthur Rimbaud: *A Season in Hell*
Arthur Rimbaud and the Magic of Poetry
D.J. Enright: By-Blows
Jeremy Reed: Brigitte's Blue Heart
Jeremy Reed: Claudia Schiffer's Red Shoes
Gorgeous Little Orpheus
Radiance: New Poems
Crescent Moon Book of Nature Poetry
Crescent Moon Book of Love Poetry
Crescent Moon Book of Mystical Poetry
Crescent Moon Book of Elizabethan Love Poetry
Crescent Moon Book of Metaphysical Poetry
Crescent Moon Book of Romantic Poetry
Pagan America: New American Poetry

MEDIA, CINEMA, FEMINISM and CULTURAL STUDIES

J.R.R. Tolkien: The Books, The Films, The Whole Cultural Phenomenon
J.R.R. Tolkien: Pocket Guide
The *Lord of the Rings* Movies: Pocket Guide
The Cinema of Hayao Miyazaki
Hayao Miyazaki: *Princess Mononoke*: Pocket Movie Guide
Hayao Miyazaki: *Spirited Away*: Pocket Movie Guide
Tim Burton
Ken Russell
Ken Russell: *Tommy*: Pocket Movie Guide
The Ghost Dance: The Origins of Religion
The Peyote Cult

Cixous, Irigaray, Kristeva: The *Jouissance* of French Feminism
Julia Kristeva: Art, Love, Melancholy, Philosophy, Semiotics and Psychoanalysis
Luce Irigaray: Lips, Kissing, and the Politics of Sexual Difference
Hélene Cixous I Love You: The *Jouissance* of Writing
Andrea Dworkin
'Cosmo Woman': The World of Women's Magazines
Women in Pop Music
Discovering the Goddess (Geoffrey Ashe)

The Poetry of Cinema
The Sacred Cinema of Andrei Tarkovsky
Andrei Tarkovsky: Pocket Guide
Andrei Tarkovsky: *Mirror*: Pocket Movie Guide
Andrei Tarkovsky: *The Sacrifice*: Pocket Movie Guide
Walerian Borowczyk: Cinema of Erotic Dreams
Jean-Luc Godard: The Passion of Cinema
Jean-Luc Godard: *Hail Mary*: Pocket Movie Guide
Jean-Luc Godard: *Contempt*: Pocket Movie Guide
Jean-Luc Godard: *Pierrot le Fou*: Pocket Movie Guide
John Hughes and Eighties Cinema
Ferris Bueller's Day Off: Pocket Movie Guide
Jean-Luc Godard: Pocket Guide
The Cinema of Richard Linklater
Liv Tyler: Star In Ascendance
Blade Runner and the Films of Philip K. Dick
Paul Bowles and Bernardo Bertolucci
Media Hell: Radio, TV and the Press
An Open Letter to the BBC
Detonation Britain: Nuclear War in the UK
Feminism and Shakespeare
Wild Zones: Pornography, Art and Feminism
Sex in Art: Pornography and Pleasure in Painting and Sculpture
Sexing Hardy: Thomas Hardy and Feminism

In my view *The Light Eternal* is among the very best of all the material I read on Turner. (Douglas Graham, director of the Turner Museum, Denver, Colorado)

The Light Eternal is a model monograph, an exemplary job. The subject matter of the book is beautifully organised and dead on beam. (Lawrence Durrell)

It is amazing for me to see my work treated with such passion and respect. (Andrea Dworkin)

CRESCENT MOON PUBLISHING
P.O. Box 1312, Maidstone, Kent, ME14 5XU, Great Britain. www.crmoon.com

Lightning Source UK Ltd.
Milton Keynes UK
UKOW05f1431160414

230081UK00003B/26/P